A STUDENT'S GUIDE TO SUCCESS

DR DHEERAJ MEHROTRA

Contents

Preface

Hi Guys

A Student's Guide to Success *is a priority learning module for all students of all ages. As we mount to the dependence of technology in nearly everything we do, we have to have the strategies to reflect on or work and learn with the march of time.*

The book entertains such a spectrum and prepares the students to mount their success ladder with mindfulness and the brilliant routine they need to follow in this VUCA world of uncertainty, post-COVID and amidst the Russian - Ukraine dispute, which has affected the global world upside down!

Happy Learning, Guys!

Dr Dheeraj Mehrotra

www.authordheerajmehrotra.com

ONE
SUCCESS VIA MINDFULNESS

As the word signifies, mindfulness imparts meaning to "The Quality or State of being conscious and aware of something". I was a teacher, quote it as MIND ATTENTIVE and aware of self under all circumstances. In transpersonal psychology or spiritual psychology, a matter commonly addressed is the thought of the self past the ego. If mindfulness is to develop into an established portion of the education of children and young folks, the most excellent standards of professionalism and evidence-based integrity must be maintained. Mindfulness in the school environment was discovered to have numerous benefits for the classroom. Some of the sought after advantages lie towards ENGAGING the children's minds towards learning and the lessons.

There are no bad or wrong means to practice mindfulness. They might originate in the classroom for some students, but that doesn't mean it stays there. If this is the case, you are practising an easy form of mindfulness by activating your five senses and looking for more information visit Mindfulness among children.

Since students' brains aren't fully formed to produce vital executive decisions, it's even more critical that educators supply them with tools to improve their emotional awareness, their capacity to slow down their thought processes, and their capacity to consider effective choices.

Keeping this in pace, schools need to offer the education and spectrum towards MINDFULNESS to kids formally. If your youngster's school doesn't have a mindfulness program, it is still possible to teach them how to become more mindful. Being a natural SPECIAL EDUCATOR or a teacher counsellor isn't just about teaching mindfulness. Scores of activities from several interests have been offered for students to select from, ensuring that every student would discover an activity they enjoy or try something new. Students welcome the chance to sit quietly with focused attention, even just for an instant. The advantages to the brain are getting more and more apparent. All the advantages that come out of mindfulness are not simply theories either. If you've seen benefits from practising mindfulness, you might want to explain the experience with your kid.

Such developments could affect the autonomic, affective and cognitive processes. The research proves that children gain from mindfulness on many fronts, including cognitive outcomes, stress reduction, and total wellbeing. Scientific research implies that mindfulness might help

repair a chronically stressed brain. Studies reveal that meditation can decrease tension and anxiety in children while boosting their attention and focus and boosting their academic performance. Notably, the analysis found that self-control isn't an absolute variable. Other studies have proven that practising mindfulness may also decrease ADHD behaviours and boost attention in young students. In addition, studies with adults imply that mindfulness may be an effective treatment for depression. Many people think that mindfulness is only beneficial for adults because adults can feel stress. But contrary to popular belief, stress can affect children, especially in school. Students experience toxic stress every day due to pressure to get good grades, an increasingly competitive environment, and the uncertainty of the future. It is widespread now to hear third-grade students say that they felt like dying when they failed to understand a subject in school or got terrible grades. This is why teaching mindfulness in school is essential. It is an important method to help students cope with stress and achieve excellence in learning.

An individual may not be concerned about what happened previously nor overly anticipate the future. Perhaps the most striking shift in the mindfulness world is how it is fast becoming an essential addition for schools that place student mental well-being near the top of the agenda. Finding time in your school day might be your main challenge—a location where folks invent things. Thinking up a set of best practices is among the things that must be done. Some folks are merely hopeless. Most people don't feel that he'll ever acquire sober, including me. Indeed, my practices towards sharing my MINDFULNESS Lessons derive interest in me to explore the MINDS of the young with readiness and an approach towards CREATIVE learning as a requisite to their personalities. The framework dwells with the inception of learning to learn as a hobby rather than an occasional occurrence in totality.

Improve Attention and Cognitive Skill

One of the biggest reasons students can't focus in class is because of a low attention span. Even straight-A students can lose focus every once in a while, and it often makes them feel bad about themselves.

Mindfulness meditation can solve this problem directly affecting the brain, especially the hippocampus. Practising mindfulness can help the students to concentrate better. And since it jogs the hippocampus to be more active, their memory and critical learning skills will improve and help them get better grades.

Develop Better Interpersonal Skill

The competition and pressure to always be the best in class can affect students' social and emotional skills. They tend to only focus on themselves and don't care about what's happening around them.

Interpersonal skill is essential to survive in the real world. So, the school must make sure that the pressure to perform well will not harm their interpersonal skills. Mindfulness training will also make the prefrontal cortex, the part of the brain that regulates emotion, more active. As a result, the students will be more empathetic, more friendly and improve their behaviour in school.

Help Students Coping with Stress

Stress is not a stranger in a human's life, and it is also very typical for students to experience stress when facing a challenging time in their education. However, the situation of the modern education system often forces the students to experience toxic stress, the kind of stress that can negatively affect their mental health.

The worst thing about this is that most students don't know how to deal with their stress. This is the most dangerous part of stress. Pressure is every day, but if the students don't learn how to cope with it, it will lead to various problems from an inability to regulate mood, impaired attention, even physical problems and depression.

School should not only focus on lessons and grades, but also education for life. The education system should start to pay attention to the student's well being too, and mindfulness meditation is one of the best methods. It will teach the students to improve their mindful awareness to help them cope with stress, improve their optimism about life, and improve their school performance. I attribute it to sharing my FREE UDEMY Lesson on MINDFULNESS for all our fellow readers. Just log on to the UDEMY app or the website and search for FREE Course: How to have quality through Mindfulness within classrooms?

The schools need to incorporate lessons on "SELF LEARNING" and "SELF KNOWING" via medication and community services as a TEAM and page at the universal approach of learning outside the walls of the classrooms for a greener pasture of gaining knowledge, wisdom and grit to do things perfectly. The teachers have a new role of being a ZEN master here and attribute their learning to ultima. The time is now! The tide is Now!

SUCCESS
go get it

TWO
Success Mantras

Dear Students,

Success is a priority in life, and it must be pursued with the march of time. As we know, every individual needs a little push sometimes. Whether you're starting on a new career path or need a burst of motivation, these inspiring #habits will remind you that success is possible. Let them be your practice and a priority in life. Happy Learning, Guys!

HABIT #1

Prepare yourself to learn: You need to be prepared for learning. Without preparations, you cannot know. If you fail to PLAN, you PLAN to fail.

HABIT #2

Gather the resources for learning: Learning involves reading, writing, listening, watching, and practising. You need to have books, notebooks, videos, podcasts and webcasting. Cash on WWW- Whatever, Whenever, Wherever learning policy.

HABIT #3

Shake off your anxiety and stress. If your mind is anxious and stressful, you cannot learn. You can know well only when your mind is at peace. Have joy while Learning.

HABIT #4

Get some exercise: Exercise helps you maintain your physical and mental health. If you are not healthy, you learn slowly.

HABIT #5

Eat a balanced diet for better learning: You cannot learn when your stomach is empty, and you will also not be able to know if you have overeaten. Eat-in short intervals but not all at once!

HABIT #6

Boost your mental capacity: To learn, your brain should function properly. Your brain will work better if you use it more. You have to use your brain to think, contemplate, and analyse.

HABIT #7

Take a brain supplement: You can boost your brain by taking brain supplements or foods that enhance memory. Teachers often suggest DARK CHOCOLATES for better memory!

HABIT #8

Sleep well for better learning: There has been numerous research on how good sleep helps better understand and analytical thinking. Rest for 8 hours, work for 8 hours but not the same 8 hours!

HABIT #9

Develop deep concentration: You need to concentrate on lessons to learn them. Without attention, you cannot remember. Explore learning by understanding the content as a story. Make use of ICT – the videos to explore the learning topic wise.

HABIT #10

Take a break to learn better: Taking a break from your everyday life boosts your creativity and mental capacity. Long study hours will not help you in learning.

HABIT #11

Explore Outdoor activities: Activities such as strolling in a garden, going for a walk or being with your pet for a while will relax you. When you are relaxed, you will learn better.

HABIT #12

Change your focus: Studying the same subject again and again will only create monotony. To break that monotony, you need to change your subject quite often; for instance, you can switch between science and arts.

HABIT #13

Reading: Reading is the most common method to learn. If you want to learn something, you have to read about it. Browse the NET, read newspapers or post on social networking. News on apps is not exceptional even.

HABIT #14

Rereading: One-time reading may not help you understand everything; you have to re-read for better understanding. The second reading will give you a better HABIT, even more, the third reading. This applies to your notes and chapters.

HABIT #15

Speed reading: Reading will help you learn; however, speed reading can better understand you. Research has proved that people know better if they do speed reading.

HABIT #16

Analytical thinking: To learn something, you need to have analytical thinking. Analytical thinking means you analyse the HABIT carefully.

HABIT #17

Learning by listening: A baby learns a word by listening. Listening is the primary method of learning. Listen before you speak.

HABIT #18

Learning from the environment: The environment is a great teacher. You can learn so many things from the surrounding.

HABIT #19

Developing interest: You won't learn anything until you are interested in it. For instance, if you are not interested in math, you will never learn math.

HABIT #20

Exploration: If you want to learn, you have to explore. Exploring means examining something, analysing it thoroughly.

HABIT #21

Research: Researching is a great way to learn. When you research something, you will know about it. Practice CURATING knowledge.

HABIT #22

Learning from elders: The elders have lived more years. Therefore, they know things better. You can learn so many things from your elders. RESPECT them, honour them and learn from them.

HABIT #23

She is learning from young ones: People more youthful than you can also teach you so many things because every person is unique and intelligent in their ways.

HABIT #24

Classroom learning: Classroom learning refers to attending school, college and training centres for formal education. Formal education is the most popular learning method. You always need a facilitator to learn and explore knowledge. Try taking the maximum through queries.

HABIT #25

Distance learning: You can get a formal education by attending schools and college. However, if you cannot participate in schools or colleges, you can still learn through distance education. Distance education refers to learning from home. Even online learning: The best option to explore via UDEMY, COURSERA, LYNDA, EDX and others of choice.

HABIT #26

Online schools: In recent times, online training and education are becoming very popular. You can enrol in online schools, universities, even training institutes to get a degree or diploma online.

HABIT #27

Learning from the real world: The actual world is the best classroom to learn various things. You have to be a keen observer to learn from the real world.

HABIT #28

Make Study a priority: To learn, you have to study. Studying does not only mean virtual/real classroom looking; studying also refers to learning by self-study. Always keep and refer to some books apart from your TEXT or prescribed books.

HABIT #29

Innovative learning: To learn, you need to study. However, you should also have the right approach to studying. It would help if you acquired clever studying techniques. Learn to browse smart. Blog your queries and showcase your social presence via putting questions.

HABIT #30

Online discussion boards: Online discussion boards and forums can provide a good platform for building knowledge and skills. Get going with your ONLINE REPUTATION MANAGEMENT by posting and hosting ability of your interest.

HABIT #31

Blogs and websites: Blogs and websites provide an excellent resource for learning various things, from simple things such as writing an essay to complicated things such as web programming.

HABIT #32

Online search: Search engines like Google can help you research any topics and provide you with resources on anything you want to learn. Use some more search engines and be an innovator and a contributor to learning through contribution to Wikipedia!

HABIT #33

Learning from videos: Seeing is believing. Therefore, you will understand better from instructional and educative videos than from a classroom lecture. Upload your YouTube videos and even comment on those you watch and share!

HABIT #34

Learning from audio media: Technology has created audiobooks; now, you don't have to read books to learn; you can listen to books. Audiobooks and podcasts are great tools for learning.

HABIT #35

You are learning from Peers. Take the best from your friends, colleagues, relatives and teachers. Share and explore the learning to the best of use and meaning.

HABIT #36

Social Media: You might be using social media for fun, but have you realised the potential of social media in learning? Get a page of your chosen topic and explore learning through sharing and re-posting.

HABIT #37

Group collaboration: Form small learners and give them something to contemplate. Shuffle the group members and let them discuss the same HABIT. Use brainstorming to generate HABITs and share knowledge.

HABIT #38

Question and Answer sites: Ask, Yahoo answers, Quora are some of the questions and answer sites that can answer your questions.

HABIT #39

Using iTunes for learning: iTunesU is an Apple platform for distributing podcasts, videos, apps, and other digital media in various categories. These media are great learning tools.

HABIT #40

Make use of the technology. Use your Smartphone Apps: On Google Play and the Apple store, you can find many learning apps. You can find these learning apps for free or by paying little money.

HABIT #41

Active learning: Active learning means the learners are involved with interactive problem solving by sharing HABITs and skills.

HABIT #42

Self-directed learning: By evaluating your performance, you can learn many things. When you analyse your performance, you will know your strength and weakness.

HABIT #43

Innovative learning: Innovation refers to creating something new through study and experimentation. If you are creative, you will always learn something new.

HABIT #44

Learning through role-playing: Roleplaying will teach you through self-direction, experimentation, and practice.

HABIT #45

Brainstorming: Brainstorming is one of the best ways to develop a HABIT or elaborate the HABIT. Brainstorming can be done singly or in a group.

HABIT #46

Interactive learning: Learners can engage with interactive learning by participating in question and answer sessions.

HABIT #47

Learning through trial and error: If you don't try, you will not know. To learn something, you should never be afraid of mistakes that you will make.

HABIT #48

Practice makes you perfect: You will never learn if you don't practice. Preparation means you do it again and again.

HABIT #49

Learning by memorising: Memorizing means repeating something in your mind again and again and recording it in your mind so that you can recall it when you need it.

HABIT #50

Learning from a storyboard: Storyboard is an excellent method of learning lessons that requires memorization and visual interpretations. Storyboard uses infographics, images, and stories.

HABIT #51

Learning from stories: If the lessons are introduced as stories, learning will not only be fun but also effective. Storytelling technique can be used for children as well as adults.

HABIT #52

Learning through stimulation: Stimulation refers to an act of arousing people to perform an action. By stimulating the learners' mind, it will be easier to impart knowledge.

HABIT #53

Welcome new HABITs: In order to lean, your mind must be open to new HABITs. With a closed mind, you will never learn new things.

HABIT #54

Learning from your hobbies: Your hobbies can also help you learn. Think about what your interests are, and then explore your interests.

HABIT #55

Learning by solving puzzles and word games: By solving puzzles you are always learning something new, it can be a new word or new information.

HABIT #56

Board games: Board games are not only fun but also helps in analytical thinking. You can play chess not just for fun but also develop strategies.

HABIT #57

Learning by playing games: Outdoor and indoor games will help the learners to think creatively, solve problems, and face challenges.

HABIT #58

School/college clubs: School and college clubs can provide a learner a platform to form a team with the peers and exchange HABITs and knowledge.

HABIT #59

Make the best use of the Book clubs: By joining a book club, a learner will be introduced to the vast knowledge contained I the books. Book clubs also provide a platform for mutual exchange of HABITs and expressions.

HABIT #60

Go by your choice. Make learning a habit. Do what you want to do: You will learn only when you love it, if you don't love science, you will never learn anything about science. In order to learn, you have to love it. When you love the subject, you become more creative.

HABIT #61

Creative teaching methods: In order to learn, the teacher/trainer should introduce creative teaching methods like introducing audio/video, using multimedia etc.

HABIT #62

Learning from newspapers and magazines: Newspapers and magazines are the sources of news, information, and knowledge.

HABIT #63

Learning from the radio: Because of its reach and flexibility in using, radio is a great source of learning. You learn a great deal by listening to informative and educative radio programs.

HABIT #64

Learning from TV: TV is a popular medium of entertainment for the people of all ages, however, you should also realize the learning potential of TV.

HABIT #65

Powerpoint presentations and slideshows: It is easier to learn when the lessons are introduced through powerpoint presentations and slideshows.

HABIT #66

Comic strip: People learn better if drawings are used to explain the lesson. Comic strips provide a better understanding of lessons.

HABIT #67

Learning through the survey: Survey not only gathers information from the participants but also helps in drawing a conclusion.

HABIT #68

Watching documentaries: Documentaries are audio-visual presentations of facts and events. Documentary helps in better understanding.

HABIT #69

Museums: By visiting museums, a learner will learn more about the history, art, and culture than by reading books.

HABIT #70

Going to the exhibitions: Exhibitions are open classrooms to learn so many things. By visiting an art exhibition, you will learn about art, by visiting a photography exhibition, you will learn about photography.

HABIT #71

Learning by writing: You lean better if you write it down. Writing is a great way to understand or memorize something.

HABIT #72

Explore Meditation as a priority. Research has proved that meditation develops mind power and concentration. Meditation is a way to tap into your inner resources and strengthen your ability to concentrate.

HABIT #73

Change your learning methods: If one learning method is not working for you, change it. For example, if you are unable to grasp from books, watch educational videos.

HABIT #74

Immerse yourself in learning: When you are learning, immerse yourself fully. Watching a TV and reading a lesson cannot go hand in hand.

HABIT #75

Lose yourself: If you are uptight, you will never have a better understanding of the subject matter. Don't take learning as a burden.

HABIT #76

Recall to understand better: In order to grasp the lesson, you must be able to recall it. You can unable to recall means you did not understand properly.

HABIT #77

Acronyms and mnemonic devices help in better understanding: Acronyms and mnemonic devices are tricks to memorize information and facts. By using these devices, you will be able to recall what you have learned.

HABIT #78

A picture worth thousand words: A picture has so many things to tell, if you can associate a picture with something, it will be easier to learn.

HABIT #79

Learning through brain map: Brain map is a way to get an overview of something. Brain mapping will help you to see the connections between different HABITs and utilize brainstorming techniques.

HABIT #80

Learning from symbolism and semiotics: If you have an understanding of the symbolism and semiotics, it will not help in the learning process, but also assist you to retain information efficiently.

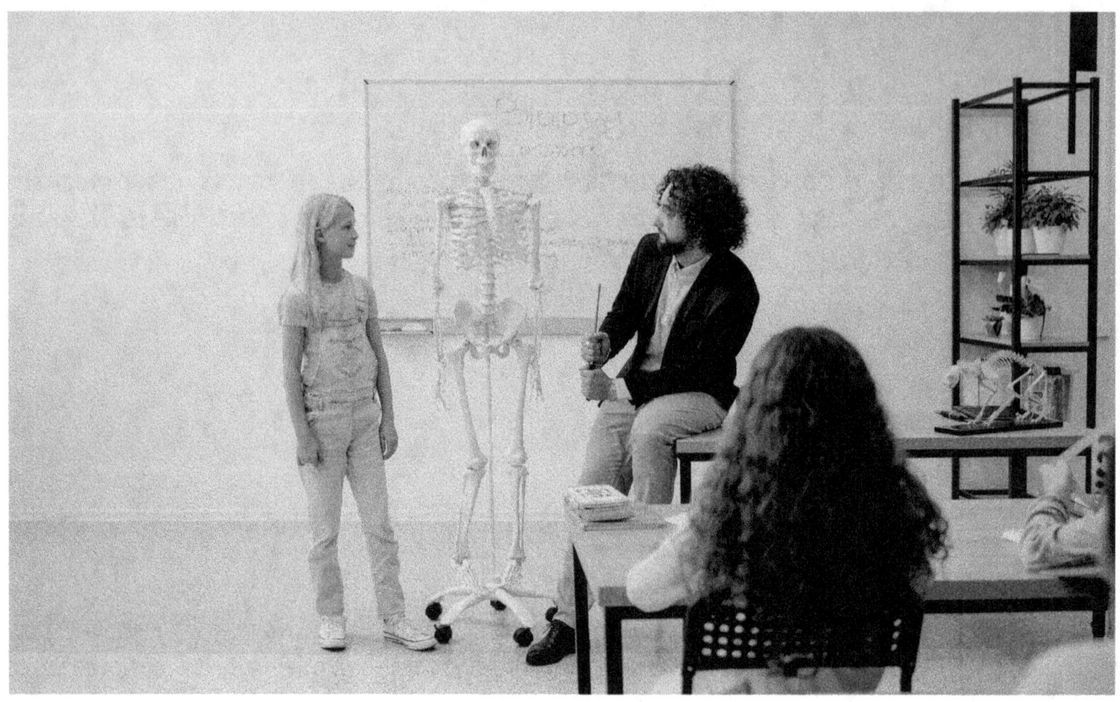

HABIT #81

Learn by mapping your task flow: Generally speaking, requires acquiring knowledge in a specific sequence. If you can organize your thoughts on what needs to be done, you can prepare yourself to complete the tasks and know "how to learn."

HABIT #82

Get inspiration: Inspiration invokes your creativity. Inspiration invokes your efficiency. You need the inspiration to become a better at learning something.

HABIT #83

Develop optimism: Optimism matters in life, even more in learning. Optimism will help you get involved in learning. You are a better learner if you are an optimist.

HABIT #84

State of happiness helps in learning: If you are a happy person, you excel in learning. A sad person or a pessimist individual will always fail in learning.

HABIT #85

Stimulate HABITs: In order to make yourself more receptive to learning, you need to stimulate HABITs. You can stimulate HABITs by playing rhyming games, using word-association, or stream-of-consciousness.

HABIT #86

Learn super learning methods: Scientists and educationists have developed super learning methods. Research on these super learning methods and use the one that is most appropriate for you.

HABIT #87

Learning through binaural beats: Binaural beats is a super learning method. In this learning method, two different frequencies are played simultaneously to produce different feelings including alertness and concentration.

HABIT #88

Always Carry a notepad: Thoughts and HABITs are like sea waves, they come and go. You need to have a notepad to record your thoughts; even your phone's notepad will work. By recording, you can easily recall.

HABIT #89

Always Keep a journal: Journals are different from notepads. On note pads, your thoughts and HABITs are basic, in your journal you can explore these thoughts and HABITs. You can add visual details, charts, brain maps, etc. in your journal. A journal will help you keep track of your learning process.

HABIT #90

Age is never a barrier: In order to learn something, age does not matter. It does not matter whether you are young or old, novice or experienced, you can always start learning.

HABIT #91

Always remember, Any time is the right time: There is no bad time for learning if you want to learn you can start learning any time. Socrates was trying to learn how to play a musical instrument even though he was sentenced to death.

HABIT #92

Dedication: Without dedication, you cannot learn. If you want to learn something, you must be a dedicated learner.

HABIT #93

The desire to learn: You cannot learn until you have the desire to learn. The desire to lean will create a passion for learning.

HABIT #94

Motivation: You need the motivation to learn, without motivation you cannot learn, or become a slow learner. Motivations also keep the distractions away.

HABIT #95

Find the purpose of learning: If you have a purpose, you can learn better. If you can find out "why do you want to learn," you become a better learner.

HABIT #96

Set a goal: Having a goal helps you learn better. You should have answers to the question like "what do want to achieve through learning?"

HABIT #97

Every skill can be learned: There is nothing impossible, you can learn any kind of skills. All you need is motivation and dedication.

HABIT #98

Exercise self-control: All of wants enjoyment in life, however, life is not all about enjoyment. There are things you should learn in order to make life better. Therefore every learner needs to exercise self-control.

HABIT #99

Learn how to learn: One of the best ways to learn is learning how to learn. Find out various learning methods and apply the method that best suits you.

HABIT #100

Learn what you know and what you don't: No one is dumb. You know many things that others don't know. To learn something you should know what you already know. You can always learn what you don't know.

HABIT #101

Become a better learner by multitasking: Multitasking does not mean you watch the TV while reading the book. Multitasking means doing similar things at the same time. For instance, you can start learning two different subjects at the same time.

HABIT #102

Apply holistic approach: You can learn better through a holistic approach. Holistic thinking is the most advanced learning technique to learn new things.

HABIT #103

Learn through repetition: In order to grasp a new theory or a new subject, you need to study again and again. Repetition will help to absorb the concept.

HABIT #104

Apply the Quantum Learning model: The Quantum Learning model uses foundation, atmosphere, environment, design, and delivery in order to impart knowledge and skills.

HABIT #105

Get necessary tools: If you have the right tool, you can learn better. Books are a primary source of learning, however, you should also use other tools like podcasts, videos, multimedia etc.

HABIT #106

Learn through critical thinking: You need critical thinking in life, even more in your learning process. Critical thinking will develop your analytical skills and help the ability to learn.

HABIT #107

Learn complex problem solving: Your ability to solve complex problems will not only help you to manage your life but also develop better learning.

HABIT #108

Engage: Learning is not just reading books or listening to the lectures. Learning is all about participating in the discussion, asking questions, and answering questions.

HABIT #109

Using information pyramids to learn: Learning process goes through various steps. Learning always adds layers. You learn alphabets, you learn words, you lean sentences. Add advance concepts to your learning pyramids.

HABIT #110

Learning from video games: Video game has a bad reputation because the market is glutted with the violent, non-educative games. However, you can find many educational games that help in effective learning.

HABIT #111

Go beyond the curriculum: It is true that a school/college goer should excel in the school curriculum, however, there are many things to learn from the real world.

HABIT #112

Learn from the real-life experience: Classroom learning is important, however, the knowledge you gather from a classroom is never enough in life. You should learn from the real-life experience.

HABIT #113

Applied learning: You learn from a traditional or online classroom, however, if you cannot apply your knowledge, you are just ignorant. Know how to apply what you have learned.

HABIT #114

Teach yourself: You should never depend on instructors and teachers to learn. By teaching yourself, you will be equipped with basic knowledge that helps in the learning process.

HABIT #115

Start blogging: Now this might surprise you. However, if you create a blog and publish what you have learned, it will not only help you understand the concepts better but also help other people learn from what you have learned.

HABIT #116

Quiz yourself: You have learned something but do you realize how much you have absorbed the concept. By quizzing yourself, you will not only find out what you have learned but also help to recall what you have learned.

HABIT #117

Learn the basic things: Without knowing the alphabets, you cannot learn a word. Therefore, start with the basic concept and gradually reinforce your knowledge.

HABIT #118

Practice Persistence: Thomas Edison once said, "Genius is 1% inspiration and 99% perspiration". Never give up on learning. Don't be intimidated.

HABIT #119

Challenge yourself: Generally speaking, you are more intelligent than you realize. Attempt to do something you have never done, you will realize your true potential.

HABIT #120

Don't be afraid of castigation: The world is full of cynics. There are people around us who always try to downgrade us. Don't be afraid of people who criticize you.

HABIT #121

Don't be afraid of failures: It is not possible to succeed in every walk of life. Failures are the part of our life.

HABIT #122

Remember to have a Party before an exam: Don't take "party" in a literal sense. Partying refers to relaxation. Cramming on the subject before the exam is not going to help you excel in the exams. Review what you have learned throughout the semester and sit relaxed.

HABIT #123

Learning from animation: Research has proved that people learn better if the lessons are introduced through animation videos. For better learning, animation should be combined with lectures and textbooks.

HABIT #124

Learning through multimedia: By using projectors, slide shows trainers and educators can make learning fun. The learners, on the other hand, are eager to learn if the lessons are introduced through multimedia.

HABIT #125

Learning from workshops: Workshop is a brief intensive course for a small group of learners that emphasize on problem-solving.

HABIT #126

Do the hard work: You will learn only when you work hard. Hard working means studying the subject matter, practicing the lesson learned

HABIT #127

Work smart: For effective learning, you need to work smart. Working smart implies using the right tools to study.

HABIT #128

Result oriented learning: Learning should always be substantial. If you are never rearing a cow, there is no point in learning how to raise a cow.

HABIT #129

Learning skills: You will learn better only when you have learning skills. You need to develop skills like concentration, reading and listening, remembering, time management, etc.

HABIT #130

Gather and assess information: If you are learning something, gather as much information as you can, and then analyze the information and interpret insightfully.

HABIT #131

Relate what you have learned: You learn to make your life better. Your knowledge is for your life. Relate what you have learned to your real life.

HABIT #132

Understand the requirement of the institution: In order to learn, you enroll in an institution. Every institution has its own requirement such as attendance, assignments, participating in the discussion etc.

HABIT #133

Think about the subject: Learning is never limited to one subject, you have to learn various subjects: Think about the subject you are studying. In a history class, think about the past events; in a biology class think about animals and plants.

HABIT #134

Look for interconnections: Subjects are interconnected. History is connected with culture and politics. Science is connected with math. For effective learning, you need to see the subjected as interconnected.

HABIT #135

Try to understand, rather than memorizing: Of course there are things that need to memorized, however, for effective learning, you need to understand. Actually, when you understand, you can memorize it.

HABIT #136

Have faith in your instructor: If you doubt your instructor, you will never learn anything from him. Your instructor is your coach to guide you through the depth of knowledge.

HABIT #137

Figure out your weakness: Find out what you find most difficult. Study the subject more, practice the lesson and develop your knowledge.

HABIT #138

Seek to find the key concept: When you are learning a certain subject, try to find out the key concepts. Once you know what the subject is all about, you will develop the ability to improve your understanding.

HABIT #139

Evaluate your listening skills: You actively listen to the lecture, do you understand everything he has said. When the lecture stops, you must be able to summarize the key points. You can do this only when you are an active listener.

HABIT #140

Evaluate your reading skills: You are reading a textbook, do you actually understand what you have read? Reading is connected with understanding. You need to understand what you are reading.

HABIT #141

Create a study schedule: For effective learning, you need to create a study schedule. Creating study schedule means you are developing a routine to learn various subjects.

HABIT #142

Combine various sources: If you are learning a subject, never rely on one single book, look into other resource material as well.

HABIT #143

Form your own view: You might be reading the notes from your teachers and peers, however, in order to excel, you need to have your own perceptions.

HABIT #144

Measure your progress: For effective learning, you need to analyze your progress. When you measure your progress, you will know what you have learned until now and what needs to be learned more.

HABIT #145

Develop emotional intelligence: Emotional intelligence means your ability to stay motivated and cope with stressful situations in any kind of learning environment.

HABIT #146

Avoid fixed mindset: You can never learn well with a predetermined mindset. If you belong to the fixed mindset, you will fixate on problems and feel overwhelmed.

HABIT #147

Growth mindset. If you have a growth mindset, you will embrace challenges and treat them as a chance to learn new things.

HABIT #148

EQ and IQ: To become a better learner, you need to have emotional quotient (EQ) as well as intelligence quotient (IQ).

HABIT #149

Don't compare yourself with others: When you compare yourself with people who know better than you, you will be discouraged to learn. Instead of comparison, focus on enhancing your knowledge on the subject that you knows better.

HABIT #150

Say No to shortcuts in life: You can impress your instructor by copying from your friends, internet or elders. However, these kinds of acts will never make you knowledgeable.

HABIT #151

Enroll in "how to learn" courses: You might learn from traditional learning methods like reading, writing etc. However, for better learning, effective learning you need to be equipped with modern learning methods.

HABIT #152

Learning is never ending process: You completed a course, but this is not an end to learning. You should continue to learn.

HABIT #153

Be receptive to learn new thing: Life is full of challenges. In order to overcome these challenges, you must always be willing to learn new things.

HABIT #154

Teach to learn: It might sound weird, however, it is true. According to a study carried by Washington University, if you teach, you will know the subject better.

HABIT #155

Don't just pass the test: The primary aim for many students is to get high scores and good grades. However, if you concentrate on just passing the exams, you will never have a better grasp of the subject matter.

HABIT #156

Make Learning a priority via sessions: According to the experts at the Louisiana State University's Center for Academic Success, learning session that is less than 30 minutes is not enough to learn the subject, likewise, if the session is longer than 50 minutes, the learners lose their interest.

HABIT #157

Taking a short break between the learning sessions: Research has shown that if you study something for a certain time and take a break and come back to study again, your brain will retain what you have studied.

HABIT #158

Using mental spacing for effective learning: In order to learn better, you have to study every day instead of reading throughout the day and never going back to the lesson. Repeating the lesson over and over for days will help you understand.

HABIT #159

Take a study nap: According to a research published in Psychological science, downtime is important when it comes to retaining what you have learned. Taking a short nap between the study sessions boosts your mental capacity.

HABIT #160

Change your learning method: Using the learning method again and again might increase boredom in the learners, whereas changing the learning methods will make learning exciting.

HABIT #161

Interact with the subject and topics: The key to learning is how you interact with the subject and topics. You need multiple sources of information and you need to interact with the information.

HABIT #162

Ditch your learning style: If it is not working for you, ditch your learning method and embrace a new one. Don't stick to books only, gather videos, podcasts, movies, and blogs on the subject matter.

HABIT #163

Make learning meaningful: You learned many things in your schools and colleges, how many of you actually remember those lessons. You remember only those lessons that actually matters in your life.

HABIT #164

Learn by doing: Reading and listening are great ways to learn, however, you should never limit to reading and listening, you also try to learn by doing it. You will never learn photography until you being to take photographs.

HABIT #165

Study the masters: Learning concepts and theories are important, however, learning who propounded the theories and concept is also very important. If you find out how these concepts were developed, you will learn better.

HABIT #166

Study the masters, practice what they have told: You need to learn how the masters' did it, however, just by knowing how they did will not help you, you need to practice as well.

HABIT #167

Learning through association: If you can associate the knowledge with something, you will understand it properly.

HABIT #168

Deliberate practice: Practice is a great way to learn. However, if you are more into the things that you already know better, you are doing it the wrong way. You need to devote to things that you don't know or do not know much.

HABIT #169

Push yourself out of the comfort zone: In order to excel, you have to push yourself out of your comfort zone. You should give more focus on things that you find difficult.

HABIT #170

Find a mentor: If you have a mentor, it is easier to get to the next level quickly. A mentor will offer you valuable perspective and experience that will improve your skills and knowledge.

HABIT #171

Be curious: Curiosity stimulates learning. You are curious mean you are eager to learn.

HABIT #172

Avoid procrastination: If you procrastinate, you are not learning anything new, or learning at a slow speed.

HABIT #173

Avoid laziness: Lazy individuals are not receptive to new knowledge and information. Laziness will make you dull.

HABIT #174

Focus on Ws' and H questions: The questions like why, who, when, where, and how will help you explore the concept for the better understanding.

HABIT #175

Summarize what you have learned: If you can summarize what you have learned, it indicates that you have understood the subject matter well.

HABIT #176

Highlight and make notes: As you read books on the subject matter, highlight the key points and make notes. A while later you can go back to highlighted sections and notes. This will improve your understanding.

HABIT #177

Right study materials: Having the right study materials also aid in the learning process. The right study materials will make your learning process efficient. The books you choose should be the best book on the subject. Books are never enough; you also need notes and handouts.

HABIT #178

Assessment through tests: If you participate in tests, you can learn how much you have learned. Tests will also show your strength and weakness.

HABIT #179

School/college camps: Go to summer or winter camp. When learning is taken away from the classroom, it becomes fun. When a study does not look like studying and is more of an entertainment, the learner's ability to understand greatly increases.

HABIT #180

Afterschool programs: Afterschool programs offer creative learning method. These programs are not just a way to entertain a child, but also a creative way to introduce lessons.

HABIT #181

Outdoor classrooms: These days educators are taking education outside the classroom and giving more emphasis on outdoor classrooms. Learning becomes effective when it is blended with real life.

HABIT #182

Learning from the community: If you are involved with community work, your emotional intelligence will improve. In order to be receptive to learning, you need high emotional intelligence.

HABIT #183

Learn by play: Maria Montessori was an Italian educator who discovered how children learn better if they learn through the games. This also applies to the adults.

HABIT #184

Learning space for better learning: In order to have a better understanding of the lesson or be eager to learn, classroom environment should also be nice. Students learn better if the classroom is well decorated.

HABIT #185

Create useful and relevant learning experiences: Individuals appreciate immediate relevancy. Therefore, learning will be effective if the learner can relate it to their lives and understand how they can use the knowledge.

HABIT #186

Focus on practicality: Generally speaking, people are not interested in learning theories; all they want to learn is how to enhance their knowledge and performance to excel in life.

HABIT #187

Learning in mother tongue: Research has shown that if the learner is allowed to learn in his mother tongue, he/she will perform better. Language should never become a barrier to learning.

HABIT #188

A sense of humor for better learning: You don't have to make serious face to learn. Likewise, the instructor should also have a good sense of humor in order to encourage learner's participation in learning activities.

HABIT #189

Suspense element for effective learning: Mystery invokes curiosity and curiosity motivate the learner. If the instructor can introduce mystery (not giving everything in the first class), the learners will be wanting to know more.

HABIT #190

Individualized learning: All the learners do not have the same mental capacity. The learners will have a different understanding of the same lesson. Therefore, for better understanding, lessons should be individualized according to the learner's ability.

HABIT #191

Know the benefit of learning: If the learner knows what he will benefit from learning this thing, he will be eager to learn.

HABIT #192

Get the experience, not just the course: learning is not all about knowing the concept. Learning is about knowing how to benefit from what you have learned. At the end of the day, the learner should get the experience, not just the course.

HABIT #193

Provide feedback immediately: If the instructor gives feedback immediately, it will have a positive effect on the learner. Feedbacks are a great way to inspire and stimulate the learner.

HABIT #194

Constructive criticism: The learner needs criticism, however, criticism should come out as constructive criticism. The learner should be made aware of his strength and weakness. When we receive constructive criticism, we attain a new perspective on how to improve from a third-party lens, which can give you the opportunity to notice things you missed before and motivate you to try a different approach to your work.

HABIT #195

Create an informal learning strategy: Learning does not have to be too formal. In fact, learning becomes more effective in an informal learning environment. One has to Learn how to make strategic thinking a daily habit, so that you can make the best use of your time, energy, and effort at work.

HABIT #196

Social learning: Learning becomes more effective when it is a collaborative exercise. Social learning will help you create a better learning experience. In simple words, social learning is the idea that children learn from observing others.

HABIT #197

Case studies: There is so much to learn from case studies. In fact, people like Darwin and Freud developed their theories from case studies. On priority, through qualitative research in the form of case studies, we tend to explore the reading habits of ours and hence can be identified as gifted readers.

HABIT #198

Create sticky notes: make notes of important points and post on the wall or notice board. These notes will help you memorize the key points. One of the highly mastered skills of successful people is note-taking.

HABIT #199

Options are necessary to excel in the learning process: The learners should have an option to choose what they want to learn. If they are allowed to choose what they actually want to study, they will perform better. We know that making healthy choices can help us feel better and live longer.

HABIT #200

Observation is a simple, yet a great way to lean. To learn something, you have to observe it systematically. Observing things comes down to slowing down to notice the small things. The quiet things. Or even the forgotten things.

Author, Dr Dheeraj Mehrotra receiving the National Teacher Award by the President of India, year 2006.

THREE

THE LEARNING CYCLE: POST PANDEMIC!

Post CORONA, we aim at a new normal. Both at workplaces as well as schools, things and expectations have changed. To the range of Understanding, Mentor and the Instructor's overview is the most compelling concern for incompleteness. The cloud computer Circumstance triggers the connection with satisfaction to learn/ share/ work together and mix the understanding training overview within colleges.

Throughout the years, with the march of time and trend, the education and learning system has provided progression to the country, and the globe as all Leading firms around the world focus and service the roles of Indians recognised for their Know-how and Knowledge.

To our satisfaction and excellence, the Indian Education and learning is honoured to the international education and learning globe for the INTENTION OF THE DECIMAL SYSTEM and the EXPLORATION OF NO. This stays our previous golden era of Education and knowing teaching Circumstances.

The ingenious understanding is not restricted to a physical room; however, an open knowing circumstance with beginning to one's convenience at his checking outhouse in your home or a Television Room at big. It is significantly unlike the course space discovering with the same team all the time, at all times. Below the neighbourhood is various as well as the knowledge is extra stunning better.

The knowing circumstance of upgrade needs a couple of required viz.

Supplying accessibility to high-quality education and learning that is functional, appropriate, personalised, and reliable.

Embrace ingenious (tech-based) methods to supply faster growth of education and learning chances to all.

Discover linking the void in between teaching and learning and employability.

Advertise social equality/economic practicality.

The paper components the activation of innovation in High Getting results and recipient contentment amongst institutions.

When it comes to carrying out the brand-new devices of understanding, the promo has produced in creating the High-quality cult in colleges these days with a range of inputs with the stakeholders viz—moms and dads, Trainees, as well as educators. Initiate clings the globe that the educators are no more the single imparters of understanding; however, they require encouraging the pupils to find out at speed and their recreation via individual knowing networks maintaining their unique attributes of skills and the rate of interests. The instructors do not wind up after the course more than yet on the shock for 24-hour around the cyber affiliation or social media networks even more. There is no wall surface currently or the limit of discovery. The cutting-edge instructor needs to initially develop an individual understanding network for their enhancement. Not just this, it needs to reach the pupils too, wherein there is no border of restriction in an effective means. It is a method to develop ones' very own class as well as one's very own network of knowing. The adjustment or the change right here is to share suggestions that are not so in the one to numerous settings of class discovery.

The connection through the cloud neighbourhood is terrific and to the reach of bulk. It appears amusing to some, yet the reality continues to betray us that the highly Indian Education and learning System is just one of the unique educational program aspects in the nation at the same level as the establishing ones. It is excellent and among the prospering with the march of establishing a society of WWW (Whatever, When Ever Before and Wherever) pressure of finding out stage by the masses. Our students today are SMART, viz. Methodical, Careful, Imaginative, Reasonable, and Skillful in obtaining the best type of education and learning. We are using the abilities of exceptional databases and society of Understanding by doing. No question, the application of ICT-based findings will effectively provide a fillip to the needed experience. The restrictions show up randomly but mirror the vibrant suggestions and possibilities using financial investments in the order of facilities, understanding centres, and mentor abilities. We eagerly anticipate an understanding centre in the nation, quickly providing rates to the international colleges. What is required is an expertise culture incorporated with a guild of learners and lectures at a typical wavelength of understanding and supplying the knowledge.

As learners of the tech age, we have a new notion now of being learners of age with the new vocabulary of A for Android, B for Blackberry, and C for Cloud. Counts for concern and a change mindset!!

About The Author

Dheeraj Mehrotra, MS, MPhil, PhD (Education Management) honoris causa., a white and a yellow belt in SIX SIGMA, a Certified NLP Business Diploma holder, is an Educational Innovator, Author, with expertise in Six Sigma In Education, Academic Audits, Neuro-Linguistic Programming (NLP), Total Quality Management In Education, an Experiential Educator, a CBSE Resource towards School Assessment (SQAA), CCE, JIT, Five S, and KAIZEN. He has authored over 40 books on Computer Science for ICSE/ ISC/ CBSE Students, over 60 books of academic interest for education excellence, and Six Sigma. A former Principal at De Indian Public School, New Delhi, (INDIA) with an ample teaching experience of over Two Decades, he is a certified Trainer for Quality Circles/ TQM in Education and QCI Standards for School Accreditation/ Six Sigma in Education. He has also been honoured with the President of India's National Teacher Award in the year 2006 and the Best Science Teacher State Award (By the Ministry of Science and Technology, State of UP), Innovation in Education for his inception of Six Sigma In Education by Education Watch, New Delhi and Education World- Best Teacher Award, BOLT Learner Teacher Award by Air India, 'Innovation in Education Award 2016' by Higher Education Forum (HEF), Gujarat Chapter, among others. He has developed over 150 FREE EDUCATIONAL MOBILE Apps for the Google Play Store exclusively for Teachers, Students, and Parents. This work has been recognised by the LIMCA BOOK OF RECORDS & INDIA BOOK OF RECORDS as the only Indian to draw that feast. Dr Mehrotra is presently working as a PRINCIPAL at KUNWARS GLOBAL SCHOOL and Lucknow in India. He has conducted over 1000 workshops globally on "Excellence In Education" integrated with Total Quality Management and Six Sigma, Technology Integration in Education (TIE), Developing towards being ROCKSTAR TEACHERS, including Cyberspace, Cyber Security, Classroom Management, School Leadership & Management, and Innovative teaching within classrooms via Mind Maps, NLP and Experiential Learning in Academics. He is an active TEDx speaker and can be viewed on the youtube TEDx channel. As a premium UDEMY Instructor, he has also developed over 450 courses and is catering to over 8 Lakh students from 180 plus countries. He can be visited at www.authordheerajmehrotra.com.

Books By The Same Author

www.authordheerajmehrotra.com

PRIORITY LEARNING FOR EDUCATORS
It is worth knowing now!
digital
body
Language
WORK ETHICS
FOR TEACHERS
TEACHER'S TOOLKIT POST COVID
TOWARDS EXCELLENCE IN TEACHING & LEARNING
200 WOW TEACHING IDEAS
NLP FOR TEACHERS
Towards Quality Teaching Skills
Teachers' Favourite Teaching Strategies That Work
Buy now at amazon.in
APPLYING SIX SIGMA WITHIN CLASSROOMS
DR. DHEERAJ MEHROTRA
EXPERIENTIAL LEARNING FOR EDUCATORS
TOWARDS QUALITY LITERACY FOR ALL
Academic Audits In Schools
What, Why & How?